ACKNOWLEDG

First and foremost, thanks to my husband and son, fo
You are both the centre of

Thanks to all the friends that have shown me support over th ...., you know who you are.

Thanks also to my Mum and my dear departed, much missed Dad.
This one's for you both, with love.

Notes:

To June

with love & best wishes
from

Ange chan
xx

TABLE OF CONTENTS

REJECTION (2011)

You left a shadow on my heart
the day you left
and went away

A shadow that eclipsed, the love that I felt
that left me wanting,
for you

And there'll always be a special place
somewhere in the deepest recesses
that will always remember you
and the good times we shared
despite your cruel departure

You left a shadow on my heart
the day you said
you didn't want me
A shadow that burned
a hole on my heart
that left me reeling
from you

You left a shadow on my heart
the day you died
and went away
The memories will always stay
for memories are all
I now have

TOMORROW (2011)

Tomorrow's dawn may never come for you, or I
Death's icy grip may be so bold
and the lacy frost may shimmer, and take hold
of your heart, your mind, and soul.

The grim reaper may strike and claim
you or I as his next victim
No longer for this mortal coil
but taken to the depths to boil
in eternal fires of Satan's dark grip.

Or perhaps admittance to Heaven's gate,
where angels wait to caress your soul with peaceful tunes
Cherubs will welcome you or I, if we've been
good in all things, thought and deed.

To float in eternal, endless skies
watching over those we loved and left behind
on firmer soil, in another lifetime,
when we were young.
And alive.

TOO LATE (2013)

A thousand "sorry's" won't dry the tears
Or make the hurt dissipate

The memory of the ugly side of you
Cannot be erased from my memory of hate

By flowers, cards and gifts
Attempting to indicate the contrary

Outwardly showing you care
Inwardly meaning it too, temporarily

Until the flowers are forgotten
And the next cruel jibe or unkind word

Is uttered in hatred
Like a shard through my dreams

Cutting cruel reality into my hopes
The roses of regret do not stop
Me from remembering

They only serve to transfer
Their meaning from love, to something else

LOVE OUTGROWN

My battle scars
They'll never find
For they are of
The emotional kind

The secrets locked within my sleep
The dreams inside that make me weep
My broken heart, I'll always keep

Images locked upon the screen
Their meaning
Unmoving, emotionless, unseen

Guilt is forming on my brow
Who can ever save me now?

Myself, it seems,
Release this torment!
And soothe me back
To lovers lament.

Words unsaid mean nothing to me
Give me your heart,
Or set me free!

MAGDALENE ASYLUM

This poem was inspired by Marc Almond's song "Bluegate Fields" which was first sung publicly at Wiltons Music Hall during his residency from 28th April to 3rd May 2008. I gave him this poem as a gift in 2009 and he later told me he thought it was "brilliant". An accolade indeed! :-)

In researching information regarding Bluegate Fields on the internet, I discovered the phenomena of Magdalene Asylums which started in the Victorian age in London and comprised of prostitutes "rescued" from Bluegate Fields. The often viewed as harsh institutions, continued to operate throughout the 20th Century; the last Magdalene Asylum closed in Ireland in 1996, and as at February 2013, the Irish Prime Minister issued a formal apology for the Irish Government's part in the running of these institutions.

Within the walls of the Magdalene Asylum
Live the ladies of the night
Dark Angels who have fallen from grace
Removed to "protect" the human race

Selected by the Government
By the Righteous and the Holy
The hypocrites who lifted their skirts
Then publicly decreed, they were nothing but dirt

In the Magdalene Asylum
Are the hookers, and whores and sluts
Women who were forced by circumstance
By a world who didn't give them a second chance

The jaded jezebels from Tiger Bay
And the whores from Bluegate Fields
In the Magdalene Asylum
They hide their secrets and fears

The women who are as sane as the day
Who touted their bodies, for men, to pay
Victorian values have no place here
And the women will always live in fear

And if they leave this terrible place
With shame and disgust all over their face
They'll return back to their old stomping ground
With a certain smile and new courage they found...
...at the Magdalene Asylum

ODE TO WILTONS MUSIC HALL (2011)

For the uninitiated, Wiltons Music Hall is the most wonderful theatre in the hidden depths of East London, formed from 5 townhouses by showman and entrepreneur, John Wilton, in the latter part of the 19th Century. It is currently in a crumbling, albeit gorgeous, faded-glamour state and therefore it is imperative to maintain this building. Wiltons Music Hall has only survived due to the love and hard work of its current keepers and has been the venue for many a well-known film, drama, and music video.

I have no connection to Wiltons other than being a great admirer of this wonderful piece of architectural history. I fell in love with Wilton in 2008 and it has been a joy to attend a variety of events there ever since.

Its history is just a small part of its allure and to secure its future, to enrich future generations of this rare gem, any donation large or small would be gratefully received. Please visit www.wiltons.org for more information.

Oh dusty walls, what secrets you keep

Within your dark hall, so much history weeps

In each brick and beam, a story of old

Sadly crumbling walls, images of faded gold

Every turned spindle, and each wooden stair

Ev'ry board of the stage, demands love and care

A music hall of such rarity

And a soul inside of such scarcity

A glamour of times past, to be reincarnated

But we have to act fast, or it will be degenerated

To retain the romance, a pledge or a gift

Donated with love, to give a much needed lift

PANTHER (2011)

Silently you creep, thru jungles dense and deep
Graceful as a dance, you leap and prance
Between trees you hide, your beauty undefined
The feline of felines, sleek and beautiful
Camouflaged from being, in a world of your own seeing
A predator of life, so skilled and precise
As you go in for the kill, your beauty haunts you still.

LONDON; An Ode to Gerry

Written in February 2013 as a gift to Gerry Potter (Poet), who originates from Liverpool and lived in Manchester for all his adult life until he made the choice to move southwards to London. I had made a similar transition in 2004, for different reasons.

What do you do,
When you're Northern
Thru and thru,
And opportunity is thin on the ground?

You make a decision,
(if filled with derision)
And pack a bag to
Old London Town.

A word of advice,
Before you move South,
The streets are not paved with gold

But a rich mix of fate,
Will open the gate,
To a life full of Sparkle and glam!

Life's what you make it
(Another cliché, its true)
And karma will have its own say

But you'll look back with glee
When you decided to be
An honorary Londoner (just like me)

You won't lose your sense
Of real Northern Pride
and your accent will always stay true

But most important of all
At the end of the day
You, Gerry, will always be you!

THE MOON (The Lady of La Luna) (2012)

Cradled in the blanket of Celestial skies
You light the way,
Ending the day
The tide ebbs and flows
To your waning heartbeat
And I fleet.

Momentarily

Your grapefruit status delivers unease,
Unsettles me,
Before your quartile self
is revealed, waning.

(A partial revealing, is more appealing, to me)

In demi gibbous illumination
You start to grate,
On my unease
Oh Please!
Madam de a Luna,
Save me from your fate
Await
Be late
and consummate
The night sky with your glorious light.

Take flight,
Be bright
and in my sight
Shine your heavenly glow
Allow the sea to flow
to the waxing of your perpetual mystery

And when the daylight arrives
You hide
behind sunbeams and rainclouds
Always there,
Unseen
Waiting patiently for the night to fall
To perform your starring role

La Luna (2013)

The moon is just a mirror ball
We are the dancers in its light
Specks of rainbow prism
Oh! What a glorious sight

La Luna shines brightly in the celestial night
In sparkling shades of silver and gold
The eternal mystery of its changing light
Is formed from shooting stars, behold!

Lapping tides on Midnight's water
All is quiet on the rippling sea.
Rising moonshine for sons and daughter
Climb to the moon and make it free

In awe and wonder you care-take the skies
A shower of stars form an epic display
And change the moon's shape to a sequinned surprise
Whilst we are sleeping soundly, and quietly lay.

(inspired by the Pixar short film of the same name)

THE LAST FAREWELL (2012)

The final farewell was a sunny March day
Oxford Circus station, ground level
The scene of the 'bon voyage' far from home

We talked, animatedly
We hugged, as sisters
We said goodbye, with love

We did not know that this was to be the final farewell on our friendship

Circumstance prevailed;
I scratched the surface of our friendship
and was left wanting.

History repeating itself
For the time we lost
and the time we will lose
I am sad.....

My judgment questioned
Your character, changed
So easily influenced by the hatred of others
Perpetuating itself onto your gentle soul
Forever the same

Je suis, desole.

SOHO (The Commercialisation of a Character) (2012)

Has there ever been,
A more changing scene.
Than on the Soho streets
In London Town?

In the 50's and 60's
It was a classy affair
A place for artists and actors
To meet

Interesting characters to greet.
A place to retreat.
For the hustlers and the men
who dared to fall in love.

In later years the landscape changed
It was a brassy affair
Where dealers and rogues
Would sliver in droves
Marking the territory
Like an alley cat.

Gangs would fight
And hatred prevail
By those to ignorant to care
About the lady of Soho.

In recent years it was a sassy affair
Women who flaunt their wares
Without a care
For the passing tourist
Eager to take a photo
To remind them of Soho
in London Town

BEACH

Crashing waves and salty air,
Kids play with a ball, without a care

Parents keep watch, or laze on the sands.
Sunscreen applied, "it's all over my hands!"

Deckchair tangle and beach hut retreat,
Lounger towels placed, "please get me a seat!"

Plastic buckets and spades that dig,
Pile it sky high and make it so big!

Castles of sand and moats of sea,
Lollies, ice cream; a 99 for me!

Fish and chips, and other such fayre,
Chip fork challenge, paper open, laid bare

Plastic pot with Seafood snack,
"Get one for me, I'll pay you back!"

Tangled hair, in sea salty rats,
Games on the sand played with cricket bats.

Seagulls' scream as they swoop and fly,
Food snatched from tourists as they walk by.

Skimpy clothes worn to get a tan,
Bikini babes bake to entice a man.

Tattoo parlours, the fun of the fair,
A day trip spent forgetting your cares.

Lovers entwined, away from the crowd,
Kids shout to the breeze, very loud

Windcheater fail as winds blow it over,
Contained within; revealed are the lovers

Coastal walks along the sea shore,
Partners hold hands, more in love than before

Food wrapped in foil and tea from flask,
Yes to everything for me! when asked

Names carved in sand (after a fashion),
It will wash away later, by waves which are crashing

A day at the beach, fun for the family.
All memories made, then sold to the sea.

BAD LUCK (2013)

Alas, Wish bones plucked from a cooked chicken carcass,
Little fingers hooked for luck.
Dandelion stalks blown to the wind
To scatter seed on the breeze

Stray pennies at the bottom of my purse
Tossed into wishing wells and fountains
And turtle backs of oriental temples.

Regrettably, Shooting stars
Darting across night skies
As a rare beacon to wish upon.

Lotto tickets, dogs, and racing horses
Odds stacked against
Yet still we hope beyond hope

Amusement arcades
Silver pennies
Dropping, falling, cascading away our dreams

Sadly, Birthday candles
indeterminate number of years
Reflected on a well meaning cake
To disappoint, annually.

Fortune tellers and soothsayers
Are mere charlatans to the truth
Defenders of reality
We believe their lies
Because we believe in the entity of "good".

The Talismen, rabbits feet and four leafed clovers
Have failed to perform their role
Despite their rarity

Bad luck in abundance
Is it karmic or Kismet?
Fact or fate?

MIDNIGHT (2013)

A misty veil hangs silently stale
Just feet above the ground
In midnight's embrace
A glowing moon face
Illuminating dark, all around

You silently race
Through streets and lanes
Your sole aim; to get safely home
For the deep of the night
Has mysteries and fright
Imagined when your mind starts to roam

The shadowy street furniture
Form imagined figures
The innocent fox, cat, other
Seeking food or shelter
Spooking your calm.

VODKA (2013)

Liquid clear
Burning nectar
nestled on ice
and a slice
A dash of lime
Satisfy my need
For delay
Of the inevitable

Feel the burn
SO welcome
Passing down your throat
Nestling in your chest
Giving you heat
From within
and without remorse

THE MOVIES (2013)

Enter the darkness, walk gingerly along
Find a seat in the void,
Feel you belong

A common objective
An experience shared
Action or drama, or horror. Scared?

The stench of stale popcorn
The shuffling in seats
The crunching of Nachos
And other vile "treats"

The slurping of syrup
Mass mixed from a goo.
The actor on the big screen
Is he talking to you?

The snogging on back rows
The irritates shushes
The seats are too hard
You're in need of a cushion!

PG or 18 who judges
the censor?
Violence or sex or
Too vile to mention.

The movie then ends
They credits they roll
You leave feeling "something"
Now real life takes toll

Real life you must enter
And leave fantasy behind
And ponder the value
Films have on mankind.

REGAL

I've snogged on its back seats
Watched movies galore
Now its raised to the ground;
The Regal is, no more

I've seen movies with dates
And film there with brothers
Bond, Terminator, Lord of the Rings
Romances, thrillers and others

It's a sad state of affairs
When a town is demolished
But my memories are intact
If my feelings are admonished

AMNESIA (2009)

Down in the darkest shadows,
Of the deepest, dirtiest street,
Near the sinful subways of shame,
You can hear the pounding of feet.
Belonging to the hookers,
Who offer you a treat,
In return for your dirty dollar,
The world lies at their feet.
For an hour of their time,
(and more than likely their soul)
They pleasure you with compliments
And what a joy you are to behold.
But you know its just a game,
Where you are not the winner.
And you'll never hear the truth,
And you'll alway be "a sinner".
For a little time later, you go,
And not pay them a second thought.
Just hand over the filthy lucre,
And try and forget all the hurt.
They don't do it for the love,
Or an element of job satisfaction.
They do it for the money!
And to live life with some added action.
And once you've closed the door,
They sign deeply and try to forget,
And return to the dark lonely street,
Seeking another Johnny to forget.

THE NIGHT (2009)

The night creeps in like an unwanted stranger,
Reeking of darkness, of fear, and of danger.
The moon lights its path, as it leads you astray,
It invites you to linger, then invites you to stay.

The shimmering stars can't protect you now,
As it creeps through the street; no escape can you keep.
The night still invades in its own darkened way,
Protecting your promises deep inside sleep

And when the first light of the morning is here,
The night is just resting; retaining the fear.
For you know in your heart; its just a matter of time
Before the night will return, and lure you into the sublime....

THE CITY (2007)

You order diamonds and drugs by room service
and the rent boys cost same as the beer
You adore the life in this city
You make your pilgrimage here every year

The first time you came to this city
You gave in to its urban mystique
The sights that you saw weren't too pretty
and it lacked a convincing technique

The streets which are laden with stories,
Of hazardous tricks in the night
And the buildings within mask a secret
That's revealed in the truth of the light

The dusty and dirty apartment
Forms the place that you like to call home
Though your stay is only a fortnight
And you always reside on your own

You invite a mysterious stranger
To spend nights of debauched fantasy
And you relish the obvious danger
Whilst experiencing sweet ecstasy

The view from the rented apartment
Is a sky-line that's tainted with sin
And the stars shining brightly upon it
Are the lights from your soul deep within

The narrowest streets veil the secrets
Of a velveteen lifestyle within
and the lush and the spacious apartment
Allows songs of the city to sing

The intimate silence is broken
By undying cries of delight
and the ghost of the voice softly spoken
Seem to fade in the deep of the night

The charm that you seek from the city
Is a truly mysterious thing
and the city you crave to deliver
Is the city of intrigue and sin

You crave the surreal illusion
Of a life that is tinged with despair
and you unleash the reign of contentment
As your journey will carry you there

The vacuum of urban denial
Fills your being 50 weeks o' the year
And you yearn for your annual visit
To experience the life you hold dear

And after your visit has ended
You'll wearily travel back home
And you'll wash the decay of the city
From your hair and your flesh and your bones

ELEVENSES (2012)

A Coffee cup.

My lipstick stain

When you poured

the dark liquid

into the vacant vessel

All was well

We drank

We spoke

Then;

All was not well

The coffee catalyst for a catastrophic admission

I left

(you)

And the coffee cup

With my lipstick stain

A souvenir

Of your betrayal

STARS (2012)

Gleaming, twinkling

In the night sky

You guide my way

Through the tricky corridors

Of streets

A celestial reference point

In the heavens

To protect and guide me

SUNGLASSES (2012)

Dark orbs of black plastic

Which shield my eyes

How I love thee

You make the daylight

Bearable

So wearable

Make me become incognito

Hiding from reality

Behind my single-vision shadowed spectacles

Life seems more real

Behind lenses of steel

And I feel

More bearable

More Care-able

More shareable

THE MORNING AFTER (2012)

Strong black coffee

And a cigarette;

Suburban cures

For the night to forget.

A night of fun,

And meeting strangers.

Slightly dark,

And laced with danger.

In shady streets

You remember liaisons

Where your drug of choice

Made you wanton and brazen

The morning after;

No regretting.

A repeat performance?

Soon.

I'll be betting.

STRANGER (2012)

I met you in a nightclub

The one of my youth

Long past visited,

When I was cocky and cool.

Revisiting, recently

Brought back youthful memories

Of fun times

Past forgotten

Memories locked away

In the tower of my mind

You unlocked that door

With your key of consciousness

And now I remember

I remember it all

When I met you in a night club

Many years ago

PERFUME (2012)

I spray your scent

Onto my skin

Is it desirable?

Am I more desirable?

Does the heady concoction

Tell you who I am

As the fragrance reacts

With my skin

It stains my cells

Impermanence

For the day,

I shall smell this way

Does it define me?

Does it refine me?

Until I wash and

It ceases to mask

The scent of me

Am I bare

Without that scent?

SHOEBOX OF DREAMS (MAY 2013)

A life full of passion, in a shoebox of dreams
Of wild nights of fun and a lifetime of schemes

Of evenings with friends, and days in the sun
A generation ago, is when it begun

My first was my hero; Numan, back in '84
at the Manchester Apollo, which now I adore

Sixteen was my age, I sneaked out alone
I missed half the gig to catch my train home

My second was my first love; Marc looked very ill
I cried all the way home, but I'm in love with him still

Memories of Siouxsie, and Mode and of others
And over the years they have all become lovers

Tickets of dates, and nights out with mates
All held in a box. With a ribbon, very safe

Each year I look, and remember each venue
The feel of the crowd; songs laid out like a menu

Every occasion has formed who I am
Now 30 years on, and I'm still a fan

More memories to come, more tickets to fill
The shoebox of dreams will live with me still

DEATH OF A GROCER'S DAUGHTER (APRIL 2013)

The streets are full of revellers
Who are partying tonight
About the death of a woman
Who would not give up the fight

The memories of Thatcher will
Always stain my youth,
And the Poll Tax and other riots
Where we all fought nail and tooth

Clause 28, and sanctions and
Of course the privatisations
She brought about a future of sorts
And the wholesale death of a nation

Her passing means nothing now
Some 30 years have passed
And I now feel indifference,
Or something else, when asked

So Maggie died today,
and I will celebrate
When Thatcherism dies as well
Now wouldn't *that* be great?!

When Tory cuts and slashes
Targeting the disabled and the brave
And Bedroom Tax for masses
Are given an early grave

When Cameron and Osbourne
Come to learn, what *real life's* all about
THEN I'll be dancing in the streets
Of that, there is no doubt

WOOLWICH (MAY 2013)

Lying in my bed
Blocking images from my mind
A bloody body lies dead
By the worse of mankind

The disturbed and the damaged
Causing havoc on the streets
Where somewhere in the shadows
A family grieves and weeps

This madness is beyond
My innocent comprehension
A knee jerk reaction
To a lifetime of tension

So where do we go now
We need understanding and love
No more death and destruction
Or "a sign from above"

The madness of the human mind
The warped feelings on our streets
Misunderstood messages
Which cannot be repeated

RIP Lee Rigby 23/5/13

WOOLWICH 2; LAID TO REST (14/7/13)

Today they're burying Drummer Lee
A nation weeps in disbelief
At the indecent act which caused his passing
The veil of sadness on Woolwich streets
How could that happen in this country, this year?
Where mad men roam and instill fear
They will not win, they have no choice
A nation speaks in one strong voice
So Rest in Peace, Oh Brave Soldier
We won't forget the life you gave
And we'll fight on against such terror
Whilst your family mourns on this sad day

FATE (MAY 2013)

Fate is a mistress cruel and hard
Unyielding ambassador for the truth
Delivers her judgement without a care
And kismet's touch will take you there

Fate gives in to karma's will
The recipe for life within her still
While intervention has its way
To change the course and save the day

DEATH BE KIND (MAY 2013)

Death be kind
Do not find
Me wanting you
Pleading you, to take me
By the hand
And lead me
To the promised land
I long to go
My body refuses
Life no longer
Does as I choose to
The choice not mine
But lays in hands
Of another deity
Beyond my control

THE GINNEL (MAY 2013)

In the ginnel of shame, where secrets lie
Where lovers hide and gussets dry
Where gossip is told and memories are sold
Where life is a story waiting to be told

In the ginnel of grime, the dustcarts pass
Through empty cans and broken glass
In puddles of dirt and nappies soiled
Starched hung clothes, waiting to be boiled

In the ginnel of crime, the gangsters hide
Stashing their goods, avoiding inside
Blue lights flash and curtains twitch
Neighbours pry and scratch the itch

In the ginnel of love where gussets fall
To the dirtiest ground, despite it all
To a nameless stranger or potential lover
The need for passion, or a bit of "the other"

In the ginnel of life all things must pass
The funeral cart will come at last
To take you away from your life on The Lane
And the ginnel of life will start again

INSTINCT (2013)

The voice within will tell no lies,
When lies depend upon the truth
Though instinct's game is cruel and hard
And shows itself long after youth.
The knowledge with age is a cruel old dame
That feeling within that has no name
The wrenching churn within your pit
Believe, deny, ignore or sit
upon the truth, you know what's right
Let peer-like influence take flight,
Believe in yourself you know it's true
For in the end what's left, is you

IT'S YOUR MUSICAL TASTE THAT I'M JUDGING YOU ON (17/6/13)

I don't care for the colour of your skin
Or the God you pray to, Or the mood that you're in
I'm not concerned if you're gay or straight
Or something between; that's not what I hate
I don't give a fig if you're a man or a woman
Active, passive, lazy or sloven
But when it comes to music, then that's where I'm at
I don't care what you like, even if its old hat
Passive popular melodies just aren't my goal
Give me some PASSION, something to stir the soul
Punk, SKA, Reggae or Rap
Something with soul, not any old crap!
Electronic, Synth, Alternative or Goth
Are where my heart lies but that's not enough!
Shades of Brecht, sea shanties, and Brel
Delivered by Almond, now they ring my bell!
Siouxsie, the goddess, is my kind of girl
A fan since the 80's, I've watched her unfurl
Mode are the synth gods, delivering sound
Which bridge the gap 'tween pop and underground
Too many to list that have a place in my history
(Some combinations, quite frankly, are a mystery!)
But forget any prejudice, traditional hates
My music is who I am, its fate
Its me, its who I've become
So please remember when its all said and done
It's your musical taste that I'm judging you on

SLAP (17/6/13)

A fist raised in anger
and brought to the face
A welt on the cheek
Leaves a mark, in its place

Then, hands round the throat
Intended to harm
A public's divided
And removed is all calm

What matters the money,
or influence?
All social decay
Starts with violence

Degrees of the pain
Matter not to the fact
Intention is all
Not the size of the act

Thin end of the wedge
In the public view
If the tables were turned
would you allow this, for you?

MIRROR MIRROR
(June 2013)

Oh mirror mirror. oh what do you see?
All lies and deceit staring back at me!
But you can't see the hurt, and you can't see the pain
So mirror mirror please look again.

Your looking glass eye can only reveal
The shell of my body, and not what I feel
Whilst deep inside your fairground friend
Sees images twisted, and the hurt that they send

Reflections of age or reflections of youth?
Oh mirror mirror, please deliver the truth!
Show me the facts, not the lies that you show,
Inside your silver secret, we'll never know

Your fragments of glass, sparkle and shine
And delivers so much to me all the time,
Your 1-D stance reflects back in three
Yet your shards of the truth give nothing to me

Oh mirror mirror please reflect back to me
The beauty and glamour that I long to see
I don't want the truth, just tell me your lies
An icon, a diva,
a shimmering surprise.

WE ARE THE MOTHERS (June 2013)

We are the angels that gave birth to the youth
The children of tomorrow, the burden of proof
We are the mothers who give love without fear
Who deliver expectations, and dry all the tears

We are the women who battle and fight
Teaching a generation 'tween wrong and what's right
We are the fighters who'd kill for our kin
Who'd die in an instance to save their kid's skin

We are the hunters who seek out what's best
Who forage for joy and feather the nest
The Amazon Queens who seek out and soothe
Who calm murky waters and improve your bad mood

We are the Mums who deliver what's asked
Who sacrifice ourselves; a true thankless task
Love given in hugs, and we always forgive
We are the ones who allow you to live

We are the Mothers who are proud of our child
Who beam at each song, each memory filed
We are the Parent who's feels so inept
Yet the location of choice when secrets are kept

We are the Mothers so proud and so strong
The glue in the ointment that binds and belongs
We are the protectors of the family's nation
The keepers of love, the true salvation

WALK OF SHAME (June 2013)

The harsh morning, after the fun night before

Feeling more jaded than you've got credit for

Clothes all dishevelled and head thick with pain

Just like you've been flattened by a runaway train

Last night's mascara and last night's expression

Far too little sleep you glide into depression

Too many drinks and too much passion with strangers

Beguilled by the night, ignoring the dangers

Your memory's fading with the dark of the night

Selective retention in dawn's early light

Awakening in surroundings completely bizarre

Sneaking away from the place that brought you from afar

No idea of your mind, or your current location

You gaze at a map, and try to find a station

Others look at you sadly, eyes filled with pity

You have no concern for them or this city

Sunglasses on, and your best party dress

You recall last night's fun, a total success!

A WOMAN'S WORTH AT WIMBLEDON (8/7/13)

So Murray's a national hero,
Wimbledon won for the Brits
"First in 77 years"
"He'll be such a marvellous hit!"

But memory's are short
And memories fade
For back in '77
Women's history was made

A woman's achievement
has been given no grace
Have we really moved on
Since Fred Perry was ace?

Misogyny rife
In this day and age
Forgotten of an era
We should be disgraced

Virginia was Wimbledon's queen
Not "that" long ago
Recognition for this please!
And less of the male ego!

But praise where its due
The boy did OK
And future games glory
Now stand in his way.

REMEMBERING AMY (2/7/13)

This poem was requested to be included in the "Album4Amy", by the organisers after they saw it on my "Ange Chan Writer" Facebook page. It was released on 14th September 2013 to mark what would have been Amy's 30th birthday. I also had the privilege to present a copy of this poem to Janis and Mitch, Amy's parents, in July 2013. Mitch very kindly contacted me afterwards to say how beautiful he thought this poem was.

In your bedroom of dreams, are miracles made
A mix-tape of favourites, 25 in all, played
A track list of a life well-lived starts in your youth
The future's before you. Amy, you're the proof

A suitcase full of family stills, tells your history
"Please don't shut me up, my life is no mystery"
"Let me be heard, in nations far and wide"
But no-one can ever know what's going on, inside

A childhood wish on a star, comes more than true
Remembering Amy, for being just "you"
A legacy of memories of an incredible voice
But your life was to end, by chance, not by choice

A world weeps, a legacy lingers, a talent lost
The music we won't enjoy, you paid the ultimate cost
We only said goodbye with words, and left our hearts behind
You'll be remembered for all eternity, in a funky digital cloud

The tears in our eyes, won't dry on their own
They need a reminder from the seeds you have sown
And the passion inside stirs emotions within
So your music plays on, with our hearts in a spin

All you ever wanted was for your voice to be heard
But your life was lived in public and you unfurled.
Gone much too soon than you really should've oughta
An Icon. A Diva. A Legend. A Daughter.

RIP Amy . Happy 30th Birthday in 2013

BUTTERFINGERS

My heart was placed right in your hands
The day your love came to town
I kept it there, it felt just right
The perfect darkness to your light

The missing piece of the jigsaw game
My life was yours, when I changed my name
You kept it safe and you kept it well
My life complete and the future swell

Then years along our love did grow
Support, love, sacrifice, go with the flow
Then suddenly you gave your heart to another
You took without asking; my flame you did smother

I took my eye off the game of love
Complacent fool that I know I am
The ball was tossed, it fell through my hands
And kismet changed my future's plans.

JUST FOR THE RECORD

Just for the record, I'm not gay
I know what they think, and I've heard what they say
I love my friends of a certain persuasion,
But sexual feelings don't come into the equation

"You're a pre-op tranny" someone once said,
"and I'd really prefer it, if you were better off dead!"
Vile, offensive, trans-phobic. Block/Delete in a heartbeat

Sometimes I'm ashamed to admit that I'm straight
But views like "that" are just what I ain't
I'm a friend of a friend of Dorothy
And for that, my friends, I make no apology
I'm a "Queer Ally", a "Fag Hag", a "Queen"
Or any other labels placed right in between.
A gay man living in a woman's body
The best of all worlds, I'd wager, my buddy!

I may not sing to a different song
But I love my gay friends and its where I belong
Fabulous, glamorous, creative, artistic
All colours are here and make no mistake
Yes, I'm not gay, I'm a straight as a die
Proud, and loud, and not living a lie

BRUISES

Darkened mark upon my skin
Telling stories of a life locked within
How did they get there?
A knock or a graze?
A hit, a punch, another phase?

An innocent blemish of accidental persuasion
Or a badge of honour worn for a special occasion
What is that mark upon your skin?
Don't ask me that I can't even begin
To answer the truth or deliver a lie
A lump in the throat and a tear in the eye
"Its nothing" you say, as you cover it over
But the feelings are out there, you're not rolling in clover

Your life, a deception, a window on the world
Will they act on the truth
Or watch you unfurl?

THE TIMESHARE BED

Another solo night, in the timeshare bed
Hubby's on nights, so, alone here I'm led
The checking of windows and locking of doors
Is all down to me, but I know the score
A routine of sorts to make sure we're safe
A house wife's duty and how to behave
Responsibility mine, but done to a script
Doors, windows, keys, glass of water to sip
Check on the boy, he 's fast asleep now
With toys all around and cheeks all aglow
Silently snoring and breathing in time
I could watch him all night, this gorgeous boy, of mine
Off to bed I reluctantly sneak
Stopping myself from one final peek
More "I love you's" and a kiss on the side
A grunted response but my heart fills with pride
Then off to my own bed, its vastness laid open
Read a book, try to sleep, this room's like an oven!
The walls closing in and I'm starting to shudder
Sleep deprivation of one kind, or another
Then finally slumbers are laid at my feet
Six hours of rest, if I'm lucky, in his heat
The fan makes a noise, a rhythmic sashay
Which cools my tired body, til the cold light of day
Then keys in the door, indicate hubby is home
I look at the clock, its early, I groan!
Another night conquered of sleeping alone
A solitary existence within my own home
Up I get, cup of tea, and morning greetings
Breakfast for three, "what are you eating?"
A 5-minute catch up once hubby's well fed
Then he's straight up the stairs, to our timeshare bed.

SOPHIE

In spellbound memory of an angel,
Who's dominion stood dark and true.
Her life taken far too early,
It could've been me, or you.

She was murdered for being "different"
For having the conviction of truth,
For being herself. For being a Goth.
Her life was the burden of proof.

We will never forget you, dark angel,
Since you exited this mortal coil.
And the passion that lives on in your memory,
Will be carried by your kindred spirits, loyal.

A legacy left of being defined
As being to thine ownself true.
And though your loss hurts, deep within souls
Sophie, we will never forget you.

There but for the grace of God, go I
With Goth buried deep in my soul.
I'm ready to stand up and say that I care,
So Stamp Out Prejudice, Hatred and Intolerance Everywhere

Tears

Tears are the words
That the heart cannot say
They flow from the soul,
Silently, without delay

They stain the glass
On the window pane
And taint our emotions,
Revealing the pain.

Tears are the words
That the heart does not dare
But their message speaks volumes
They ask you to care

"KISMET"

"Give me your hand
And cross it with Silver
Before the secrets untold..."
Life and love, truth or lies
Are all waiting to be told.
Some word are reality
And some fabrication,
The number of children
Or initials of relations.
How long will you live?
And how many times wed?
When is it the time that you'll wind up dead?
Why feel compelled for a stranger to tell,
What your life will unfold, be it heaven or hell.
What fate belies us,
Depends on our Kismet.
And no one can change time
Or alter what is meant.
When its our time, fate will behold
And it isn't predicted via Silver or Gold
Life is a mystery
Which is part of the glue,
And your life is for living,
How it's done, is up to you

"The End"

On gossamer wings, the angels sing
Of purest gold, with the love they bring
The feather formed from good intentions
And deeds of joy too pure to mention
A silken dream whispers on the wind;
The gateway to the truth.
No lies are spoken.
No spell is broken.
The landscape's magic forever true
When seraphim angels are coming for you.

"Trust"

Upon my back, an angel sits
To guide me in my ways and deeds,
Their jigsaw wings, a perfect fit
And I place trust in where fate leads

"House of Cards"

Your life is like a game of cards
And once you held the flush
Parties, glamour, name in lights
You lived the life; relished the rush

Then the phone stop ringing
When a scandal came your way
An innocent party; mistaken identity
You were the one who had to pay

Today's headlines; tomorrow's chip paper
Mud sticks and you pay the price
Failed ambition becomes your karma
You live on the roll of the dice

A few drinks later, your career is a mess
The phone doesn't ring and you're less than impressed
The fragments of talent are starting to fade
You look in the mirror at the mess you have made

You once had it all, now it's gone, it's true
And what's left at the end, is the product of you.

"So Near, and Yet So Far"

A legend with name up in lights
Taking first class flights
Sampling all delights
Best of all to behold
Telling stories, bold
Rising, rising whilst others fold
They stay at the top of their game
For a while, things are the same
Then a downward spiral takes hold
Not quite so bold
You slip out of the mold....
Years pass
Public forgets
Glamour remains
Fame is the ship which has long since sailed
A faded star; you travelled so far

"The Vodka Angels"

Do angels drink vodka?
Well, sometimes they do,
Through rain or through shine,
And in morn's early dew.

The alcohol angels,
With wings spun of steel,
And a heart made of wire,
To touch, love, and feel.

The emotions of mankind,
And a barrier against haters,
They radiate tough love,
And repel all the fakers.

The fuel of the liquor,
Makes their journey time slicker,
And puts life in a haze,
which makes it go quicker.

The crystalline liquid,
Is a secret to compare,
For angels and vodka,
Are a combo so rare.

So next time you stamp,
on a creature divine,
Remember the name,
That you tread on is mine!

A Valentines Wish

Hope you got the Valentine wish
That you were hoping for,
Did you get a bunch of roses
Or cards cascading through your door?

Are you hoping for an evening
Of romantic gestures and signs
Ignoring all the clichés
Especially that "Love is Blind"

Are you hoping for some smaltz
Being whisked around the floor?
Or maybe a little waltz
As long as you aren't ignored.

Maybe you hope for lingerie
And an evening spent in bed
It's better than watching TV
And being on your own instead

Whatever you choose to do
Remember love is eternal
It's not for just the one day
That turns "love" into being commercial

And if you don't get
All that you hoped for on this day
Remember to love yourself
In the end, it's the only way!

"Soul Sistas and Soul Brothers"

The circles that you move in reveals the person that you are
The lengths that you will go to, tells the story from afar
The people that you love and the friends that you have chosen
The ones that watch over you, and those who's hearts are frozen
The test of friendship comes when the loyalty has past
And who will speak up for you until the bitter last
Who will pass the muster and reveal themselves as true
The ones who'd put themselves out, and love you for being you.

"Judgement"

You're not the friend that I thought you would be
You lied and you cheated, and you really hurt me
With duplicity displayed at the drop of a hat
I think more of myself, than to be friends with that

You're not the person I thought that you were
You pretended you liked me, pretended to care
But when it came down to really being a friend
You showed your true colours, to the bitter end

You're not the person I even want to know
Your falseness, your lies and inability to grow
I misplaced my judgement, the error is mine
So go from my life, without you, I'm fine

A Girl on a Train

Take a good look
I'm just a girl on a train
And all of my dreams
Have been sucked down the drain

Alone here I sit,
In my own little world
My tunes are plugged in
And my life is unfurled

Sunglasses are on
So you can't see my eyes
For they're filled with emotions
Of bitter despise

My eyes hide the truth
That lies deep in my soul
But they're shielded from you
So my tears won't unfold

My ego is shattered
But life still goes on
I'm going to a place
Where I know I belong

So take a good look
At the girl on the train
Her dreams are now dust
You'll never see her again

"The Angel Versus The Devil"

On Angel's wings, I hear you sing,
The joys of life, you always bring
On devil's horns, You keep me warm
With all your tales, of wicked scorn

Chorus :

The Angel versus the Devil,
The voices in my head
From good, to bad, to evil, instead
The Angel versus the Devil,
The voices in my mind
Leading me astray, from all Mankind

Contrary emotions tell me what to do,
I'm torn between the bad, and the good in you

Those Gemini Twins are taunting me
I shake me head, please let me be!
This indecision of haunting me
I shake my head, please let me be!

The Angel versus the Devil,
The voices in my head
From good, to bad, to evil, instead
The Angel versus the Devil,
The voices in my mind
Leading me astray, from all Mankind

Little voices on each shoulder
Good is winning, but bad is bolder
I turn towards the devil's horns
The angel cries as her wings are shorn

My ears are closed to all decision
This torment drives me to derision
I walk away, its not OK
My conscience deciders are here to stay!

"Lemons"

If life gives you lemons
Then what would you do?
I'd make a paella
Or put them in a stew.

A nice gin and tonic
Could be the order of the day
To remove all my troubles
With every sip; they'd float away

A nice piece of fish
With a lemon surprise
With tea and with bread
And a big bowl of fries!

Perhaps make a tart
With a nice lemon zing
With a dish of whipped cream
And some wine, that you'd bring.

So if you're lucky enough
To get a citrusy treat
Don't make lemonade
Life's for living. Now go eat!

About the Author

Ange Chan was born in Lancashire and subsequently lived in South Wales and Cheshire before settling in Hertfordshire, where she currently lives with her husband and son.

In June 2012, Ange gave up on the corporate world after 26 years, to concentrate on her writing.

Her poetry has featured in a book of photographs entitled "Winter Dreams"(with Peter Parkinson) its sequel "Winter Dreams 2" (with Samantha Reynolds and Peter Parkinson) released in early 2014. Additionally, a specially commissioned piece featured in "Visual Poetry" (photography by Peter Parkinson).

*Ange has also collaborated with photographers **MoGeo Photographic** to produce a unique series of photopoetry, available to purchase from http://www.redbubble.com/people/mogeophoto/collections/251961-photopoetry-by-mogeo-photographic-and-ange-chan*

Her previous work has been published over the past 25 years in a variety of publications and websites. In July 2013, Ange performed one of her short stories at "Polari", on London's Southbank stage to a paying audience.

"***Observations***" is Ange's first full poetry collection.
It embodies themes of love, life, and the darker side of the emotional spectrum.

To contact the author :

Twitter @angechanwriter

Website http://vodkaangel22.wix.com/vodkaangel22

Made in the USA
Charleston, SC
30 May 2014